CHAMBERSONIC

OTHER BOOKS BY OANA AVASILICHIOAEI

Poetry

Abandon
*Eight Track**
Expeditions of a Chimæra (with Erín Moure)
feria: a poempark
*Limbinal**
We, Beasts

Translations

The Faerie Devouring, Catherine Lalonde
The Islands, Louise Cotnoir
Medusa, Martine Desjardins*
The Neptune Room, Bertrand Laverdure
Occupational Sickness, Nichita Stănescu
Readopolis, Bertrand Laverdure
The Strange Scent of Saffron, Miléna Babin
The Thought House of Philippa, Suzanne Leblanc (with
　　Ingrid Pam Dick)
The United States of Wind, Daniel Canty*
Universal Bureau of Copyrights, Bertrand Laverdure
Wigrum, Daniel Canty*

* Published by Talonbooks

CHAMBERSONIC

Oana Avasilichioaei

TALONBOOKS

Talonbooks
9259 Shaughnessy Street, Vancouver, British Columbia, Canada V6P 6R4
talonbooks.com

Talonbooks is located on xʷməθkʷəy̓əm, Sḵwx̱wú7mesh, and səlilwətaɬ Lands.

First printing: 2024

Typeset in Avenir and MBF Minimal
Printed and bound in Canada on 100% post-consumer recycled paper

Cover illustration and interior design by Oana Avasilichioaei and Leslie Smith
Interior photographs and drawings by Oana Avasilichioaei

Talonbooks acknowledges the financial support of the Canada Council for the Arts, the Government of Canada through the Canada Book Fund, and the Province of British Columbia through the British Columbia Arts Council and the Book Publishing Tax Credit.

Library and Archives Canada Cataloguing in Publication

Title: Chambersonic / Oana Avasilichioaei.
Names: Avasilichioaei, Oana, author.
Identifiers: Canadiana 20240381831 | ISBN 9781772016260 (softcover)
Subjects: LCGFT: Poetry.
Classification: LCC PS8551.V38 C43 2024 | DDC C811/.54—dc23

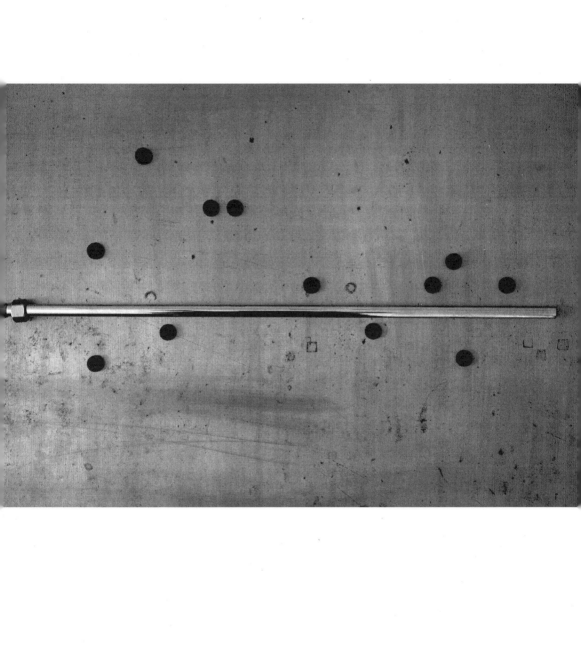

*from the very moment any voice is conceived whether
physically realized or not
manifested or not
to the very moment (if & when) delivered*

   —Theresa Hak Kyung Cha

*sounds are first of all written in the air with an exquisitely
acoustical ink*

   —Aldo Clementi

*So you've just got to keep on keepin' on. Be subversive,
very subversive.*

   —Pauline Oliveros

CHAMBERSONIC INTRO : FELLOW STATEMENTS

(an audio work & lathe-cut vinyl
imagined from Fellow Statements, Fellow Murmurs, 04:48)

Breath The closing of the door transforms the sound studio into a cocoon. Soft light demarcates its edges, while at the centre stands a simple installation: a small table, chair, recorder, and two vocal microphones. The outer world seems unfathomably distant in both time and space.

Having warmed up her vocal apparatus, she attempts a few initial breaths. The day's experiment: a vocalization of breath. Always staying on the verge of pitch, keeping to the edge of tone. Sounding out on the intake of air, on the discharge of air. Finding breath deep at the back of the throat, then deeper, down the esophagus, the thorax, all the way to the diaphragm. A breath made with the whole body that stems from the deepest depths. A breath so abyssal, it surprises the vocalist with its existence.

The purity of the recording quality in the studio cocoon (no interference, no underlying hiss, no windy chatter, no random clicks) makes the mouthful of breathy sound more concrete, palpable; she can almost reach out and touch it. It fills her body. It fills the room.

The vocalist tries out different tempos, varying the volume, the attack, the dry/wet textures, translating the curve of the palate, the soft ripples at the back of the throat, the muscular movements of the tongue, the smooth, bone-hard obstruction of the teeth into sonic breath.

The body as autonomous instrument, self-generating, self-playing. The body as its own sound chamber. The body discovering its idiosyncratic accents through breath.

CHAMBERSONIC :
ECHOES

Voices will one day ignite and spill over, fill in new fractures. They will not retract but keep on spilling.

Some voices will tingle as they unravel the linkages and lineages of lexicon and grammar.

Some voices will promontory. They will will and favour.

Other voices will attract converts. They will shift the tone of the hour from frequency to oscillation.

Others still will be placed on the pyres of history to burn and burn and burn but they will not burn out.

Some voices will congregate in substrates, they will blur and frolic.

Some voices will develop methods for manoeuvring around obstacles – linguistic, i.e. political; societal, i.e. commercial; geographical, i.e. industrial – in other words, methods of survival.

Others will cry out, not just in pain, which they will do plenty, but also in wonder at sporadic glimpses of what they will call "beauty."

Some voices will volatile, they will periphery and ricochet to centre, doubling back and shuffling forward to reach some version of substance.

Others will be neighbourhoods. They will verdant, coalescing in assemblages, they will disturb.

Others still will pander to the profits of word commerce, showing off their tectonic midriffs, their alluvial weathers. They will recline in easy chairs of conformity, addicted to hefty doses of virtual stimulation.

Some voices will speak in code or what appears as code. They will be the ones least understood but also the ones most worth trying to decipher.

Some voices will allocate the embodied moment, lived experience, risk of presence to mere trivia and ephemera.

Others will fight for the right to abstraction, its vital importance to critical thinking, to full being. They will delineate the perils of its forgetting.

Some voices will papercut. They will draw blood, from bodies, from foliage, from structure, from digital clouds, from corporate governments, from avatars of nation states.

Some voices will encompass and eviscerate. They will trace new maps that instantly become obsolete.

Other voices will sandstorm and current and tornado. They will bicker over the boundaries of ethics in armed conflict.

Others will be aquatic, atmospheric, subterranean, extraplanetary, lunar.

Some will be detritus, debris, dust.

Some voices will filament, emit a glow. At first, this will be read as a disturbance, an imposition on so-called standards of decency. But voices will filter and drain, they will drape over and bog, then marsh and wade through.

Others will vestige and amber yet refuse to be specimens. They will be exemplars only of themselves.

Come winter, some voices will disband and burrow underground. They will seek out hot springs and headwaters, they will dormant.

Some will crack.

Others will bellow.

Some will negotiate.

In a daze, in a dousing, in a descent, voices will wander. They will fortify their follicles and amass.

Some voices will village and valley. They will gather and crimp at the edges, then scatter.

Others will trip over borders. They will mole and drown over them, wall and war over them, they will ambush.

Some will extract.

Some will flute and funnel.

Some will migrate.

Other voices will go extinct. Become a footnote in a book, background noise in a recording, a rumour, an urban legend, a memory on a random blog. Some, however, will leave no trace.

CHAMBERSONIC :
LET FORM BE ORAL

Movement I

let form be oral   a foundation
of phonemes

       sonorities

are
dis
tri   bu
ted

              an impossible lone sound

corporeal   phon-

                                    recording

reassemblages
pho-
-netic

fragments   (the ghost of sound)

soni-   voice, noise, utopic hiss of dissolving
-guistic belonging

                      (phoneme as phantom)

song		
a	in disguise?	
word		
grating		

record isolates   while sounds are played

(while sounds are relayed)	(record resonates)	acoustic
		phenomena

                                                                            jangle

pho to		chains
na		of
		pitch
ry		

                              to

ry
ra
o

(a lingual tip)

                              utterances

pronunciations
linguals

organs
timbres

This is a setting on music.

audio loop	culling
	from the totality

frequency   intensity   duration

for instance

	the sound
	of swallow
	(bird)
	(ingest)

culling

	from the instant
intensity	
frequency	
duration	

		of
	totality	
swallowing		sound
the		

duration	instant	
of		
sound		

the swallow		intensity
	culling	
	with	frequency

in the process	of sound
ensnared	

voice
of timbre

or timbre
of voice

(fills the void)

traffics
the activity   of sound

louder

higher	and
l o n g e r	
(and quieter) and	shorter
lower	

where
differentiates
silence

rain	moan	wind	
whisper	sea		sound as itself
chorus		breath	
brook			

resonance

	a	profound	
	centre		off-kilter

a material	
sound	
silence	
a material	

This is a sounding of silence.

( )			
( )		(	)
(( ))	((	))	
( )		((	))

	a somatic acoustic
a proliferated density	spontaneous activated
a lived density	intoned forgotten sung
live	reassembled necessary

density

		sound			
	by		and		
		silence			
duration	shared				(says Cage)

this sharing		primordial	
		foundational	(says a voice)

the presence of		the	of presence
absence		absence	

yet tired of	dualities	
	binaries	

let's collide them p	
o	
e	
n!	

ion

s e n s e (s)

new

		evolution		
	progress			
against the linearity of				
				and for the

	multi	coalescing		n	
concurrent	direc		a		
tio		dis b	i		dialogical
nal			nd	g	

(responsive)

			of
f			
	l	o w	

	voices		
		creatures	
	ideas		impossibilities
		beings	
	plants		

This is a manifest of now.

a   ca ll i n g

<table>
<tr><td>process</td></tr>
<tr><td></td></tr>
<tr><td>not purpose</td></tr>
<tr><td></td></tr>
</table>

<table>
<tr><td>often</td></tr>
<tr><td>so yet</td></tr>
<tr><td>simple ignored</td></tr>
<tr><td>so</td></tr>
</table>

<table>
<tr><td>not</td></tr>
<tr><td>purpose</td></tr>
<tr><td></td></tr>
<tr><td>process</td></tr>
</table>

<table>
<tr><td>often</td></tr>
<tr><td>forgotten reiterated</td></tr>
<tr><td>so</td></tr>
<tr><td>though</td></tr>
</table>

<table>
<tr><td></td></tr>
<tr><td>it bears</td></tr>
<tr><td>repeating</td></tr>
<tr><td></td></tr>
</table>

<table>
<tr><td></td></tr>
<tr><td>not purpose</td></tr>
<tr><td>process</td></tr>
<tr><td></td></tr>
</table>

only   process

in

n

in   full   x   a

e   s

its   p   e

c l a m o r o u s

in   its

s i l e n c e s

can one

truly begin

to listen

to   things   in themselves

an interval   an aggregate of

motions

instruments

urges

disharmonies

                    l   i   of
sounding   t   n   things
                u   e   but
        the   physical   o

    also   t
                                        l   i
        their   their   e   v   u
                                        o   o n

        depth

This is a variant of being.

						scape
	as			as	substance	
	palpable					
context			volume			

			for a situation	
			or event	

				o	
context		ex	l		
	as	p		s	e
				i	v

	demure			
				un
		contained		
				stable

context	lating		
trans			
forming			
mitting			

	the		
		event	
situated			

	we		to		
here	you				temperament
they	come			or	
			density		

		weather		
effects	of		on the	
				material

	frailty	
	human	

	mechanical	
		causes

accidents			
			ence
	temporal	ter	
		in	fer

	b		
intentional	i		y
il		ili	
leg		t	

				reading		

		ional				
un	conv				in a	
			ly			
	ent					

			o			
				o		
		l				
				p		

			e			
		c				
			y	l		
		c				

l	f		r		r	o		n
p	a	u	p	o		p	o	t	o
	y		o	s		p	s	i
	l		p	a	l		i

composing		that	
		has	
instance	work	only	
for	a		beginnings

for
only
instance

a	
instance	that
for	

beginnings
for
instance
composing

instance	has
for	
work	

instance

beginning
a

for

This is a pause not necessarily of silence.

Movement II

```
                                    t i
                      the      u      |        takes
      s a m p l e d            m      p
                               |      e                        rolling
```

```
                                    r
                                    o
            rolling                    |    |
                                          i
                                    n      g
```

```
  listen                                              cut
                                      to      the          of
```

```
                                 of
              raw            fact
                   naked
```

```
               the        sounding        is   a    good
    whether
                                          is    real
```

```
                                    (sometimes          obvious
          u n m i s t a k a b l y          painfully)
```

m n

i		i
e	a	e
ter		
n d		t

centre

a

a	s	c
of		p
negotiation		e

ind

eter	s
mi	n
nat	gi
e	mar

an   out

integration
of

liers

nate   betw

inde	ness
termin	
	ee

	migration
trans	
a	mediation

alism

structure	method	form

ically   .

rupture

r e	ve	.
e x	i	m o
x p s s		o r
e	e	r p hol

log y

over   a

tone		e
of	f	u
	f u	u
under	u u	g

e   y   is   t u

r		s
u	i i	r
rupt r e		
u	m	m m u

cal   p

dd   r r r

d		
d		o
o o oo	t t t h	m m m m m
h h		

This is a chorus of pitches.

	u	
u		
e	e	u
		e

ear-to-ear

				(h)	(h)
	but	instance			
not			to		
note-to-note		instance			

	v		r e v erb		
v	a e			(to)	
a e w				br e v e r	
w t o					

s i	i f		g n	
g n	g n ic a n		s i	
a l	s i		(to)	
to	c e			

	the		the	prefigured
eter	n g			
m i		prefix		figuration
ind i n				

iteration

—

(—)			)))
((—))))		— —	
(—		—	
)		—	—)))

b r r e e e a a a a t t h h h
b r e e e e a a a a t h h h

This is an expression of sequence.

```
                              i
                    s   n                              e
         ter                o                p     i        s
      en                        c                c
an        coun       of                   s      e
```

```
              the
              acoustic              lim
                        sub        e
```

```
                                              emerging
   the                                merged

      guttural              sub
                    depths              submerged
```

```
               quen cy                for
         fre                       gotten
    colour                    fre
         of                   quen      goed
   the                        ted              ignored
```

```
            s   d                    m
               r   e                s
(a) l i v e      p              f       r     f
        im    o            o     m      o        r
            v i           r              o
```

```
                                                                swarm
   echo                                                              of
     echo                              behind
     echo                 word                  word           contra
            of  the                (before)   the                    diction


                              e                            ( (
                         v     s            ( interior )              ) ) )
            voice           w    r                      ( ( (
    a                 s    e                         ( (    ) )


                                        out              into
        u c               a                        we
    fl    tu    es              we         of            a
          a t      into                                              . . .
                              a


                                                             noise
                 they              the           foli      of
    sym                      into                  age           language
        phonic                                dense
               plunge                                      ( brut  bruit )


                                              b    r    u    i    t
          brut                            brut

              b  r  u  i  t


                        b         u            e
                        r      m
        brève        b    r    u    m    e              e         e
                        r
                     b         u           e
```

This is a continuation of process.

```
        n    ll      lin                              g
      li   g  o  i     l   g            gro              n
        l    r   n   o    r o       in   l        lli
      o          g r    ·  l      l       l      ro
      r                       lin   l       i   g
rolling                              gro          n
```

it's getting late   tied

```
                      the
                                                -
                    m u s i c                          a
                              tongue              this
                                                  ness
```

```
                                                  temp
                                                  orar
```
                                                    ily

    s e p a r a t e   organ
```
              from              vital
                              and                of
```
                                                  life

a s u d d e n
```
                                            assical
          contempo            a
  a                          sterpiece          ofound
    vein          of        an
```
        of   aster   emporary
                                                  uman
                                              in all of
```
                    that  there
    so that   what                          now this
            what   the
                                              the  over
```

```
┌─────────────────────────────────────────────────────────────────────┐
│  what if one   continued              using  only  what    came    before? │
├─────────────────────────────────────────────────────────────────────┤
│              (kept going)                                             │
└─────────────────────────────────────────────────────────────────────┘


                                                  m       a       n
┌─────────────────────────────────────────────────────────────────────┐
│    i c    st                    d  d                              'n  │
│ s s  i c    st              d  d                                    n │
│    s         st     d  d               e   n    n    n              n │
│    s                                                                  │
└─────────────────────────────────────────────────────────────────────┘
              st                                          u

                         ep        ·                               l
┌─────────────────────────────────────────────────────────────────────┐
│              e p              i t   a   l    i   t                    │
│     e p   a r r        a                    t                      l  │
│ e p                       a   r  r    i    a          a      a        │
│          r  r       a                 l              l                │
└─────────────────────────────────────────────────────────────────────┘


          o  n  g
┌─────────────────────────────────────────────────────────────────────┐
│                         u                                             │
│  o  n  g              u   e   u            n  n   g           i l      │
│       o  n  g         u   e   u   e                                   │
│  o  n  g                    e   u    e                        e r     │
└─────────────────────────────────────────────────────────────────────┘
                                       e

              o m        o u n d
┌─────────────────────────────────────────────────────────────────────┐
│       o m                                                             │
│ o  m               o u n d          o m                    n d   nd   │
│    o u n d                              o m                           │
│ o  u  n  d                  o u n d                        n d   nd   │
└─────────────────────────────────────────────────────────────────────┘
                                   o u n d

              an echo?
┌─────────────────────────────────────────────────────────────────────┐
│       will  it   be          a reverberation?                        │
├─────────────────────────────────────────────────────────────────────┤
│                              a transformation?                        │
└─────────────────────────────────────────────────────────────────────┘
                              a mirror?
                              a methodology?
                              an afterpresence?
```

a gimmick?

a cheap trick?

a lack of inspiration?

a process for process's sake?

This is an earful of forms.

yet   inside   something is happening
        the mouth

                                but happening
perhaps
                                        all   the   same
                    of   hearing
    below   the threshold

        tide

theatre   disharmony   synchrony
        declivity   osmosis
aggregate   mnemonic   rays
        crystal   cosmos
constellation   spasm   serial

                forms   ready   waiting   available

                                                    surfaces
                                                    volume
                    confluence   interpreter   space
in the   influence   action
        bet   performer   receiver
        ween   idea   object
c o n t i n u   u   m   composer
                    listener   event
                    transducer

[37]

it's getting late, isn't it?

it's getting acoustic   it keeps   forgetting

the   importance

it's dissolving

(   )

(   )

of silence   (   )

(   )

rs

it   u

because   c   o   gives s   to

of how   o   t   h   sound

n   ape

it keeps   forgetting   to

d i s s o l v e

d   i

s

(   )   s

(   )   o l   v

(   )   e

it's   getting   late, isn't it?

look up

the past is staring   back   at   you

This is an interval not necessarily performed.

Movement III

question

which   will be the first to dare communicate?

the communicating question

. certainly not the ~~right~~ question

~~productive~~

~~discursive~~

is not necessarily a question   generative

will   music   make   things   clear?

music will make music

will make environment

(or at least clearer?)   will make time concrete

will make space volumetric

by music   sound   will make overflow

I mean to say sequence

spillage

static (or evolving) volumescape

by music

I mean you attending (listening)

mingling your breath heartbeat electrical flow

with mine

in sharing our silences , are we making music?

This is a confusion (assemblage) of subject positions.

[40]

a palimpsest of our questions

is the music

today I saw a question

yesterday I saw music

did I become musical because long ago I was told that I wasn't musical?

or was I told that I wasn't musical so that later I would become musical?

is the sudden insertion of the "I" in these questions

an interference?
a way of going in circles?
a strategy for avoiding what's really important, i.e. the music?

of course there are rules
of course "I" "you" "we" "they" mean to break them

for example, by ~~writing~~   in the intervals   in the gaps
~~being~~
· sounding

once boundaries become oppressive, should they be ~~moved~~?

~~broken~~

(like these lines)   ~~pierced~~

reimagined

is this a truth?

are some boundaries always needed so that we can understand

form   scope   volume   "that" from "not that"?

or is boundary really an illusion?

(an idea maintained, nourished out of need)

meanwhile, still refusing to write (i.e. make music) within the lines

yet the lines keep appearing en masse

what if I receive them as non reflective?

essentially

transforming

linearity into

angles and crevices of

an anechoic chamber

will the sound just keep sounding?

when there is direction but

no reflection

will it become infinite?

will it reach a kind of eternal state?

can we then refer to it as immortal?

will that make the sound less or more precious?

will it make it more meaningful?

will it make it more beautiful?

or will it make these categories

(beauty, meaning, etc.)

neither here nor there, i.e. irrelevant?

will the sound at last be liberated?

surging in the absence of music

you might call it a preamble

I might call it an inter~~mission~~vention

they might not call it anything at all

but simply a becoming

in the chamber of contemporaneous

conflict absence loss destruction

the sound of what is alive and grounded

beckons

~~This is not necessarily an ending.~~

[44]

BRIDGE

CHAMBERSONIC :
LET FORM BE AURAL

(a sound performance based on Chambersonic :
Let Form Be Oral, Movement I, approx. 15:00)

Variation Attempt again. Click fast-forward, make drone of recorder motor. Equalize, i.e. play with the highs, lows, and mids to sculpt the sound. Its matter evolving through the air inside a room, a hall, a gallery. Having warmed the voice, attempt loops. Phoneme as phantasm. Building the sonic space through attrition, juxtaposition, accumulation until the space is saturated, maximized. Stop.

Begin again in the wake of the just heard event, in its phantom power, in its lingering aural taste. Press play. Make drone with motor of cassette Walkman. Structure now dawns to repeat. Yet not exactly repetitive. Not fully improvised either because the structure attempted, tested in advance, i.e. rehearsed. In French, *rehearsal* is *répétition*. To rehearse is to repeat. Playback. Yet never entirely identical. The goal of this rehearsing, this repeating not necessarily to perfect but rather to increase the piece's generative potential, experiment with its range of possibilities. Keep ground unstable, capable of surprising. A groping in the dark of sound. Especially when live.

The work drones on. Where silence is deferential. Skipping needle, scratchy stylus thus evoked. Mechanisms of old tech haunting the piece, rippling its waves in rippling waves, haunting the mechanism of the voice, its guttural spurts, its failed pitches, its struggling enunciations. Contact mic touching presence. Appearing to favour a rhythm of threes, break the pattern by attempting fourths or fifths. While also realizing that after the third pass, things can get muddled, risk becoming undifferentiated soup. Still, it's worth the risk.

Attempt again. Press play and fast-forward or rewind and rewind. The motors and their drones panned. A left-and-right conversation. A fluctuating feedback of responses. Breath as bridge. Space filled with reverb. That could extend forever, incrementally shifting. Until someone presses stop.

CHAMBERSONIC :
EPISODES FOR AN
ABSENT FILM

(an eight-channel sound installation interpreting
Chambersonic : A Graphic Score, 27:37)

Instrument breath, brushes, cables, cardboard box, chopsticks, contact mics, letter opener, metal wok cover, mixing console, paper, pencils, pine cones, plastic fork, processed theremin, reverb pedal, ruler, straw, untuned prepared piano, vocal mic, wood cube, zither.

CHAMBERSONIC : A GRAPHIC SCORE

CHAMBERSONIC : LIVING SCORES

Voice Scree

the voice is a score t e v ic is a core th voic s a scre e o ce s sore e oi ei a   o e
the voice is a scar th v ice s scr te o cei a s ar te vie is sca e oi ei a   a
the voice is a scree the voi s a s ree t e oice i a sc ee te voi e is scr   e oi ei a   ee
the voice is a radical e oice is adical he voi i a rad cal e oi ei a a i a
the voice is a scream t e vo ce s screa th o ce s cream e oi ei a   ea
the voice is askew the voic s skew he v ic s ask w t e vo c i aske e oi ei a e
the voice is autonomous, sacred t e vo e is aut nom us, sacre e oi ei au o o ou , a e
the voice is constantly silenced he oic s co st nt y silen d e oi e i o a y ie e
    and thus made sonorous
    the weakest of signals
    feedbacking into a roar
the voice has no substitute th voi e as o sub ti ute te oi e a o u   iue
the voice is a stage t e vice i a age he vo ce s tag e o ce i a st ge e oi ei a ae
the voice is a saga e voic s sag te vie is agate o ce sa aa e oi ei a aa
the voice is never safe th vo c is n ver afe th oice s nev r sa e e oi ei ee ae
the voice is radial the vo ce s radi l te voic i dial te vic is rad al e oi ei a i a
the voice is symbiotic he oice is symb oti th v ice s ym otic e oi ei y io i
the voice is rebellion e v i e is rebel ion te oce i ebel on e oi ei ee io
the voice is mutation, a living score he vo e is mut ion, a liv g sc re e oi ei u a io

Sonic Plain

Somewhere on a solitary plain, a body stands, a voice articulates. Sends fragments of sounds in all directions. There may be someone within earshot. The field is public after all, a sort of commons. No one seems to be listening. Or many are.

A glitch in the fantasy.

The field need not be empty, though a voice feels isolated, even lonely.

The plain, in fact, teems with life. Fumbling, crawling, burrowing, and slithering, organisms produce a deafening roar. For those who stop to listen. For those who pay attention. For those who lend an ear. Tune the frequencies. Respond in difference.

To be a multivalent subject of ear and mouth, of attention and breath, of idiom and voice. Not just multilingual or polylingual, but interlingual, crosslingual, extralingual.

Could mean to struggle against the atrophy of connectivity and being. Wander in a matrix of sound in which everything is materially connected through sonic vibrations, every reverberation touching, bouncing off, intersecting and merging with others. Intimate, physical. Both a chaotic assemblage and a generator of patterns: islands of sense, sediments of conjunctions and diversions, temporal palimpsests of volumes and tones.

To embrace the chaos, the disjunction and the connectivity. To pronounce and listen oneself into being. To bear the responsibility of the audible and the inaudible. To always begin in the middle.

Could mean to drown out the dominant voice by celebrating the unheard, the quasi-silent, the barely discernible, the almost invisible, the dissonant, the ignored, the rejected.

And in pronouncing, risk discomfort and be socially disharmonious, break the unspoken rules of politeness, the social conventions of engagement.

Somewhere on a solitary plain, a body attends to audible presence as a voice glitches, enacting existence.

Fellow Statements, Fellow Murmurs

Fellow statements, fellow hungry mouths, fellow introverts, fellow inner voices, fellow dynamic duets, fellow quiet revolutions, fellow unheroic holograms, fellow calls to justice, fellow pacts, fellow linguistic migrants, I call on you. // Fellow bonds, borders, and bodies that won't be silenced, fellow bones that won't be disappeared, fellow fierce rattling and unshackling, fellow divergent voices, fellow dissidents and discordants, I call on you. // Fellow tantrums and episodic madnesses, fellow imaginary voices that refuse to be forgotten, fellow phantoms, fellow ghosted and silenced, fellow unsung marginals, fellow musical mastodons struggling against extinction, fellow rejects, fellow ephemera, fellow notes, notations, marginalia, magic markers, fellow believers and non-believers and disbelievers and beyond-believers, I call on you. // Fellow murmurs and fissures, whispers and cracks, rumblings and time gaps, fellow articulations and disarticulations, fellow thoraxes and tongues, fellow dreamers, mystics, and visionaries, I call on you. // Fellow mispronounced, mistreated, misunderstood, misengineered, misallocated, misinformed, misrepresented, I call on you. Pronounce your part.

Street Speak

CHAMBERSONIC : IMPROBABLE THEATRES

Illusory Theatre

In the late hours of night (or early hours of morning), they enter a vibrational space. The room (if indeed it can be called a "room") is large, square, and features an interminable ceiling, walls scarred and scored by (perhaps years' worth of) accumulated sonic indentations, and a murky floor they can almost sink into. The room (such as it is), while not full, is not entirely empty either; an allegorical presence hovers in the air (which isn't exactly "air" but more like a viscous atmosphere of longing). The light is dim, as though suspended in that fleeting moment before dusk becomes night or night becomes dawn.

Upon entering, they know instantly that they will never belong to the space and yet feel an almost violent urge to remain. Gradually, it becomes evident that the walls are not solid but rather layers of semi-transparent screens: backgrounds (or foregrounds) for a play of shadow and light, transmitters (or receivers) for a dialogue (chorus, monologue, voice-over) of sonic material. And on the other side of the screens, all around, are the performers (or so those who have made their entrance initially think), their indistinct shapes moving and gesturing with a pulsating presence, as though (silently) pointing or (silently) clapping or cupping their mouths to (silently) boo and hiss.

Those ushered in (ostensibly the audience) therefore find themselves in the middle of the space (arguably centre stage) and on display performing for those behind (or rather in front of) the screens. Their entrance signals the start of the performance. It remains unclear whether their exit will signal its end or even how or when they will be able to exit.

Speculative Theatre

This play always begins at the end and ends at the beginning. Its performing space is spherical and in constant motion. The performers and spectators bounce inside it like balls in a bingo machine until one is randomly selected and extracted from the sphere, i.e. the performing space. The play ends once all spectators and performers exeunt (via this random method) and the sphere is left empty.

Theoretical Theatre

This theatre aspires to be pure dialogue.
Between a speeding train and the horizon.
Between the method and the prop.
Between ambient and monophonic chant.
Between a chorus and the extras.
Between a fragmentary interlude and a buttressed citizenry.
Between a failed metaphor and a desire to believe.
Between the megaphone and the gag.
Between the chatter and the conversation.
Between a mountain pass and some lambs.
Between a body's gestures and the floodlights.
Between the margins and the edgy.
Between the action upstage and the acts offstage.
Between the undertone and the utterance.
Between the backdrop and the spilled ink.
Between the riotous and the listened.
Between now and now.

Jeu de Théâtre : Act Antig

Enters the scene.
Avec la gravité propre to speech yet favouring silence.
With a strange smile.
With a foreign vitality.
With a gravelly voice.
Sets down a douce stylus.
Suddenly a murmur.
Then another douce implement, if possible.
Through clenched teeth.
Sits near a source, i.e. a spring, its muffled jet surging in spurts.
Sometime later.
A moment remains closed.
Then continues in a lilting tone.
Adds in a hard voice, with a shrug of their epaulettes.
An instant rests, saying nothing.
Then commences as though playing the lute.
Avec la voix comme a blunt instrument.
Sometime late.
Detaches her regard from her surroundings.
Closes the window, sits on a small stool, picks up an old, torn map
                                    from the floor, obeys a kind of stupor.
A page enters from stage left.
A garden materializes, then its brutal counterpart.
As though in jest, a gesture lines stage right.
It's at this moment that the Chorus exits.
Looks at her hands full of earth.
In a voice as if pitiful.
In a time turned reflexive.
The page and its silence confront each other.
A face refutes upstage.
Murmuring as though to herself.
The reproaches and regards downstage.
The soirées arm in arm.
Sometime lately.
Forced to stand in the midst of a heavy chamber.
Facing the deafening advance.
Something shakes (a head, a hand, a leaf).
Something is forced out.

Something else is à bout de forces.
Then in supplication.
The Chorus returns out of breath, moving erratically as though
                                                    sleepwalking.
A portal opens.
A humble terrain is sudden.
Exit Chorus.
Then a hundred paces offstage.
Their dull thuds fading in the distance.

Theatre Obscura

This theatre is a monstrosity, a locus obscurus. Inside is oblivion, a voided chamber with no sense of direction or time. Its entrance is a small aperture (i.e. a lens) through which a scene or viewer can pass. Yet, the entry also triggers an inversion and reversal upon the theatre's retinal wall.

In itself, the theatre holds nothing but a projection of an external fragment, as no action, movement, performance is possible in its interior. Such acts can only occur outside while their Platonic reflections, their phantom flickers, are upturned and made visible for an instant or eternity inside.

This theatre can be conflated with the eye, and its vision can be said to be a matter of perspective.

As the theatre is scripted entirely by external events, it can either be described as ironic or subject to forces beyond its control.

This theatre is a prompter's box held in suspension until the breath (i.e. the image) of a souffleur can activate it, making the theatre the quintessential signifier. Otherwise, it lies dormant, a tabula rasa awaiting animation.

This theatre has no beginning, middle, or end because any exterior scene can be projected ad infinitum onto its interior surface or its floodlights can stay dark indefinitely.

Ultimately, this theatre might be said to be a plane to the side of existence.

Jeu de Théâtre : Act Resist

In a garret facing
afterwards before the gates
and finally within the precincts
(alone she pens)
(blows on the screen)
(blows on the wood)
(tosses down her tools)
(she calls for help)
(several women pitch water over some old arguments)
(addressing one of the officials)
(officiating over the assembly)
(suddenly a skirmish)
(addressing the women)
(threatening them)
(drenching her with chatter)
(drenching her with simulations)
(drenching her with misinformation)
Several days are supposed to have elapsed
(addressing)
(pointing)
(vociferating)
(coming back with a soup pot)
(coming back with a frying pan)
(coming back with a megaphone)
(coming back with a placard)
(coming back with another frying pan)
(marching onwards)
(addressing)
(marching onwards)
Finis

Theatre Oblique*

Dramatis personae
OM (Oblique Motion)
OO (Oblique Order)
OL (Oblique Line)
OS (Oblique Shock)

The stage consists of two enormous verso/recto pages, slanted at a steep angle as though the stage (i.e. the "book") is about to be closed shut or is just being opened. The characters seem to have (permanently) fallen into the gutter and are struggling to extricate themselves by using various (linguistic) strategies and (more or less effective) tactics.

OM: I think we need to catch this blank terrain unawares. So maybe you three could vibrate in a line while I veer off in unexpected directions.

OO: No, no, we should push forth as one and by sheer strength of repetition obliterate all opposition in our path.

OL: You're all awry. We should create a slant, a type of ladder, and gradually attain some sort of edge.

OS: Or we could simply rock and vibrate ourselves into a frenzy until we create a shock wave that propels us out of here.

They all mumble and dither while pondering these options.

OO: I've always admired brute force. I mean, why are we in this if not to conquer?

OM: To offer alternatives? To stray from the standard path?

OS: Hmm, maybe, but there'll always be forces (like this interminable page) confronting us, trying to overpower or lead us askew.

OL: So we push our way through the mire at an angle.

In turn, they attempt OM's strategy. They fail. They attempt OS's strategy. They fail. They attempt OO's strategy. They fail. They attempt OL's strategy. They fail. Dejected, they slump further into the gutter.

OS: Let's take sharp turns.

OO: Let's make a fist.

OL: Let's go slanty.

OM: Let's stray.

Time passes. A minute. A few days. Some months. A year or two ...

OL: What if we move, i.e. write, as though building a ziggurat?

OS: Been there, done that.

OM: In going from the synthesizer to the modulator, vocables jar like electricity.

OO: Is conflict a given? A bare necessity?

OM: In listening to the chaos, we become productive.

OS: Or at least reverberate into new patterns.

They all look up to the far reaches of the stage in unison.

OL: In time, the architecture, i.e. the syntax, will become overgrown with foliage and vegetation, i.e. its music. We could see this as a new form of symbiosis ...

OS: ... a confluence of difference that ...

OM: ... we can scale to the upper ...

OO: ... edge and then jump off into ...

ALL: ... the unknown, i.e. exeunt.

*A brief foray into the standard definition of oblique (via *Merriam-Webster*) yields: neither perpendicular nor parallel, inclined (as adjective); not straightforward, indirect or obscure (also as adjective, but more metaphorical); devious, underhanded (also adjective, but darker, more ominous); a line or a muscle or a slash (as noun). The idea of the slant and slanting, the askew, the awry and the crooked, the lopsided and the tilted, off-kilter. The oblique case (linguistics), oblique motion (music), oblique type (typography), oblique correction (particle physics), oblique order (military formation), oblique shock (gas dynamics). The "standard" turns out to be more convoluted, varied, inclined in several directions.

Acoustic Theatre

The play occurs entirely sub aqua. The container of the submergence is changeable (aquarium, pool, pond, lake, fjord, ocean) and dramatically alters the experience and essence of the play. An array of underwater loudspeakers stands in for the performers. To enter the subaquatic volume, the spectator is equipped with a hydrophone and obliged to dive in or float or descend. No specific instructions are given to the spectator regarding the hydrophone, other than inviting them to explore the aquatic environment in any way they like. The play may be performed for one or multiple spectators, as its theatre is self-generating.

Upon diving into the submerged environment, spectators may float in one spot or agitate or swim or sink to the bottom. The sounds of their motions are captured by the hydrophone and transmitted through the speakers. The sounds are muffled, elongated, abated, prolonged by the water. The ebb and flow of their frequencies, the very movement of their waves and subsequent displacement of the water's volume constitute the performance.

As such, the submerged environment showcases a theatre of sound itself, of its physical properties. The spectator can decide to leave at any time, indicating the end of the performance.

Variation: An additional set of hydrophones may be concealed in the container and their recordings broadcast through the speakers, thus adding an acousmatic layer to the experience.

Democratic (Self-Service) Theatre
(after Allan Kaprow)

Upon entering the performance space, each person decides whether they wish to play the part of the performer, the viewer, or both. Any space can be designated as a performance space. Its designation as such is what transforms a *space* into a *performance space*.

Each viewer decides the vantage point from which to watch the performance, the degree of attention they lend to the performance, the duration of their viewing experience, and the physical conditions of that experience (i.e. whether they are seated, reclining, standing, lying down, suspended, etc.).

Each performer decides the type and number of actions they wish to make, the duration and timing of those actions, whether they will involve speech or singing or vocalizing or none of the above, whether they will interact with other performers or not, whether they will improvise or be directed, and where in the space the performance will be situated or move.

It is possible (in fact very likely) that conflicts will arise between a performer's decisions and a viewer's decisions, or a viewer's decisions and a viewer's decisions, or a performer's decisions and a performer's decisions. For example, a viewer might decide that the duration of their viewing will be twenty minutes, while a performer might decide that the duration of their performance will be twenty seconds. In such instances (in fact in all instances), both will need to figure out how to handle the consequences of their decisions and the impact they have on themselves and others. In the example provided above, the viewer will need to process any emotional reactions they might experience, such as feeling short changed, and how they will spend the remaining nineteen minutes and forty seconds, among other things. The performer will need to process the expansive intensity of delivering such a speedy performance and a potential sense of dissatisfaction from the viewer, among other things.

Those who decide to play both parts, that of viewer and performer, will need to negotiate between the parts, which may very well turn into multiple parts. They will also need to process any disparities, contradictions, cross-purposes, conflicts, or resonances that might arise from such a multifaceted (some might call it fragmented) position. The resolution or acceptance or rejection of these disparities or contradictions will itself be a performance.

The play ends when a consensus is reached between the viewers' decisions and the performers' decisions.

Jeu de Théâtre : Act Shakes

Dawn. A promontory.
Enter.
Exit.
Enter.
Exit, chased by a bull.
Enter.
Exit.
Enter.
Exit, chased by a moose.
Enter.
Exit.
Enter.
Exit, chased by a racoon.
Twilight. A prolonged gong.

Theatre Lucida

You enter the theatre only to realize that you've always existed here.

The space and air, the forms moving (or floating?) within it, are prismatic. They seem so intimately close, you reach out instinctively, trying to touch them, but your hand comes away empty. You think they might be an echo of the distant. Or its holographic reverse. Are you the end point or point of origin? you wonder. Probably neither.

The prisms, or their refractive effects, are made of movement, as though coming into focus or moving out of focus, yet the focus remains elusive. You begin to feel dizzy. Overcome by an increasing (and ever more unpleasant) sense of vertigo. You start spinning. Or the space does. The ambient air thickens and is suddenly blinding.

You achieve stillness. Perhaps because you are floating. Or because you pass out. Or because you are dreaming. Or because you've shifted dimensions. Or because you've materialized time. Or because you've refracted yourself.

You try moving your legs, and they seem to obey you. Somewhere to your right, you notice a fold, a type of opening, a possible exit. You move towards it and, eventually, step through.

You expect almost anything: an open sky, a busy urban street, an English garden. But then you understand that you've simply slipped into another theatre.

Jeu de Théâtre : Act Rec

A city block in ruins.
Atop a mound of rubble, an improvised scaffold.
A hanged man swings lightly in the evening breeze.
A crowd enters and crowds.
The smell of sulphur permeates the air.
Then a rumble, a flash of lightning.
Two gods enter, dressed in grotesqueries, as though on their way to a
                                                masquerade ball.
The crowd suddenly collapses, as though on command.
The light turns spectral.
One god snaps two fingers.
An instant ice storm.
One god yawns.
Nothing happens.
Then a terrible scream, somewhat echoey and tinny, is heard from the
                                                direction of the hanged man.
The gods approach the mound, stumbling awkwardly, encumbered by
                                                their costumes.
They peer into the face of the hanged man.
Instead of a mouth, a miniature recorder.
Playing a loop.
Another terrible scream.
Then a crack.
The scaffold, heavy with ice, collapses over the gods.
Another tinny scream.
Fade Out.

CHAMBERSONIC : SOUNDPACE // EAVESDROPPING ON THE PROCESS OF A DILETTANTE COMPOSER

(on the making of Chambersonic : Episodes for an Absent Film)

It begins with desire. A longing for what is yet to be conceived. Faint and fragmentary glimmers of ideas, sound heard in the mind's ear: elongated resonances, long drawn-out frequencies advancing and receding in waves, layers, reverberations // static, silent extensions // sometimes sparse, sometimes full // a sea of glass, a more active, rougher sea of surf and foam and wind // plucked chords // long vocal vowellings fading into breathlessness.

It began years before with the dilettante's desire to learn something about sound and music (because unschooled) by drawing (with an instinctual, untrained hand) a series of graphic scores. Each a drawing in itself. A blueprint of potential. A visual musicality. Perhaps a future sounding. Or perhaps not. In part inspired, urged on by the drawings, abstract scores, and sonic word riffs of New York artist and writer Nico/ Moina Pam Dick et al. And even before that, it began with the excited feeling and compelling aural images stirred by the graphic scores of some of the early experimentalists, such as John Cage, Cornelius Cardew, Pauline Oliveros, and Iannis Xenakis.

The dilettante has read that pacing in compositional music has to do with selecting the tempo and overall rhythm for the performance of a score. Pacing in sound work, and certainly in the dilettante's sonic essay, might then entail the apparent rate at which aural events take place, apparent because the sound, though transmitted rather than played, is still actively constructed in each moment by the types of speakers through which it is conveyed, by the space in which it resonates, and by the listening ear-body (with all its particularities) and the location of that ear-body in the resonant space. Pacing thus shapes an aural elaboration in space and time, yet the contours of this elaboration remain, to some extent, porous or in flux. So one composes the simultaneous evolution and nowness of these aural events, knowing that there will be variations in the impact of their pacing. So one composes with a certain (and arguably naive) sense of trust and a conviction of inevitable failure.

It began with the staff, the five horizontal lines that structure the com-position of notes (in Western musical notation). It began with the lines because of the dilettante's aspiration to draw sound though unable to read music. Thus, the five lines of the staff would be made into markers of sound.

Much later, after enough drawings had accumulated, after a selection had been made, after a potential order or movement had been established, it began with translation. From the visual two-dimensionality of the page to a volumetric spatialization of sound across eight speakers (the dilettante still called them "speakers" then, though a more accurate word would have been "monitors"). The arrangement, spacing, length, thickness, shape, proximity, colour, and texture of the lines would combine to suggest various gestures, qualities, volumes, tones, and frequencies of sound.

Thus far, the dilettante had only ever worked in stereo. Although she was a long way off from exhausting its possibilities, over the years she had grown somewhat comfortable with its qualities; its potential for structuring audio had become familiar. The leap from stereo to octophonic was oceanic. Everything she had learned (often by scrambling in the dark) had to be unlearned and then learned anew. How sound would behave within and beyond the eight-source circle. How certain shorter, more staccato sounds would remain localized to one spot, moving out of it ever so slowly, while more melodic, elongated resonances would quickly fill the room.

Pacing here was suddenly so much more complex than anything the dilettante had ever previously considered, for it was multidimensional, multifractal, a constant choice between a stationary point and a movement, between a solo, duet, trio, chorus, or a combination of all, between a focus and a dissipation, between a fullness and a fast wave, a fading and a rhythmic beat, between a circular progress and a linear expansion; all choices simultaneous, all choices exponentially increased by a factor of eight.

At first, the dilettante tried to assign an "instrument" to every aspect of the lines, a time frame to every drawing. However, this quickly failed, and it became evident that she must build the piece holistically. For every segment, she wanted the person who stood in the middle of the room of speakers to feel as though they were standing in the middle of the drawing. In certain segments, some of the qualities of the lines would be more present while others would be more muted. The duration and pacing of the segments would vary. Sonic lines, linear soundings, fading reverbs, growing distortions, washes of sound.

The dilettante selected, reselected, selected again, and chanced upon her instruments: the wet sound of a processed theremin, the raw melodies of a prepared piano somewhat out of tune, the noisy textures of various objects and drawing implements captured with contact mics, the distortions of an old zither, an improvised gong, the vocal spectre of the breath. A sense of a trace, of bareness, a shadow or suggestion of something more concrete yet that remained just out of reach was at the core of her selection.

There is a skill (which the dilettante could barely graze with her fingertips) to knowing when to let loose and when to hold back, when to add and when to remove, when and how to sculpt silence, when to build on or continue or devolve or work against what came before, when and how to be aleatory, when to defy expectations created by a particular moment and surprise or when to deliver on those expectations, when and how to make peaks into transitions and transitions into endings.

It began each day with a listening session of the whole, with note taking (such as: use theremin with reverb but no volume on theremin so record only the wet // use fainter "paperdraw 33" for lighter yellow parts of the lines // record textures: cat brush, pine cones, chopsticks, plastic fork on paper // create longer transitions // maybe extend "zoom 28" so fade-in is longer // maybe warp "texture 18" further // bring back a sound, altered or unaltered), with ideas for changes, for the next, with listening to potential sound already recorded, or with recording more. It developed slowly, drawing by drawing, second by second, in multiples of channel combinations. There was a semblance of form and of building, but also of disintegration, suspension, a tense promise of what is to come, a memory of what has not yet happened.

About halfway through the process, the dilettante asked for some feedback, a few trusted reactions on the work thus far: a sense of being out of time, out of space, prehistoric // spectral presences, eerie, lurking soundings yet largely falling between as most of the sounds can't be placed // begins in a more intimate, contained space, then moves outward, later returns to another, more intimate space embodied through a rotating, almost centripetal breath, then moves outward again, ever more outward // a sense of structures and shapes // sometimes very abstract, material, textural, other times more suggestive of images, atmospheres, figures, almost painterly // an organic machine // cinematic // electronic with much organic physicality // the dissolution of radio static.

Then the process went on, the work evolved, morphing ever so slightly with each change, addition, deletion, failed direction, progression, moment of attention. Though a semblance of an ending was eventually reached, the aural labour continues. It begins again and again and again. There is much refinement to be done, the intricacies of the pacing, the activation of the volumes, and the embodied reactions of the ear-bodies to be reconsidered. The octophonic work might only ever be completed in a moment of listening, once it has entered and reverberated off an individual ear-body in a particular space. And then in another. And then in another. And even then, will it ever truly be finished?

BRIDGE

CHAMBERSONIC :
VOICE SCREE

(a vocal audio work anticipating Voice Scree, 01:00)

Constraint Tending to work in long forms, the constraint of the minute appeals. Yet when sixty seconds are constructed second by second, the minute ends up representing a much more dilated time. Periods of expansion condensed into milliseconds. Short and sweated out. Stretched. Stuttered. Stereoed. Brevity fattened up.

Wherein the voice is split or multiplied across several parts. Some activate the foreground. One assumes (or refuses) centre stage. Some parade from left to right, right to left. While some are busy in the background, sputtering textures.

A sort of list is fused with what sounds like a classic structure of intro, bridge, conclusion. Wherein the bridge is the hinge in the poem (still to be inscribed). Antithetical structures butt heads, i.e. are at odds with each other, creating dissonance. Before you have a chance to settle into it, it's over. Unless you click play again.

CHAMBERSONIC :
OBLIQUE THEATRE

(a filmpoem based on the script of Theatre Oblique, 03:41)

Dialogue

Dramatis personae
Figure 1
Figure 2

F1: I've been trying to consider the fundamentals of theatre.

F2: In other words, a lost cause.

F1: To animate a dialogue, are actual bodies needed on a stage?

F2: Nope.

F1: That sounds very decisive. Care to explain?

F2: You need voices, sure, but voices can be disembodied. And one voice can be multiple, act more than one part.

F1: But doesn't the voice, in its very essence, always refer back to the body?

F2: Not when you think of it as the agency by which a point of view is expressed.

F1: I saw this play once in which the performers' bodies remained unnaturally still while their faces were fully animated. At first, something about it seemed off, but soon I realized that all the faces were in fact 3-D projections, and there were no live bodies on the stage. It got me thinking. To this day, I'm not sure I would still call this "theatre," since live performance was entirely eliminated from it.

F2: The *live* part was gone, clearly, but it was still a *performance*, a *representation* staged and activated in a physical space to create a particular effect.

F1: But if we remove both body and liveness from theatre, which, it seems to me, have been fundamental to it since time immemorial, what are we left with? A mockery of theatre? A cheap imitation? A quasi memory of it? A mask?

F2: Maybe something even more fundamental: a theatre unmasked. A staged array of agencies choreographed to draw us into their imagined world and hold us captivated.

F1: Or alienate us further. Like everything else in this world seems to be doing more and more.

F2: Well, like I said, a theatre unmasked.

F1: Hmm, can we agree to disagree on this one?

F2: Have we ever agreed on anything?

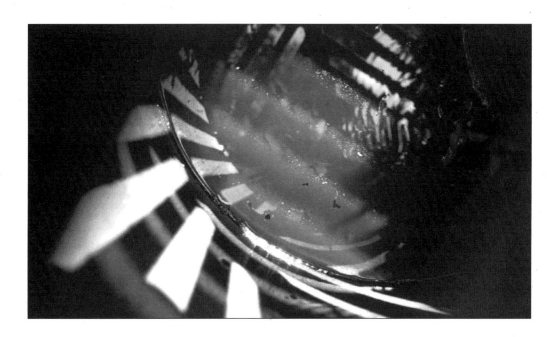

CHAMBERSONIC :
ELECTROECHOES

(a sound performance transforming
Chambersonic : Echoes, approx. 10:00)

Audience From the lit stage, most of the recently renovated basement venue reaches back into obscure darkness, faces blending into an opaque void except for a few near the front.

This audience is a bureaucrat and his entourage of assistants, clerks, photographers, and journalists. They depart after the first set has barely finished, leaving behind a few compulsory handshakes, photo ops, and some bewildered stragglers, the performers essentially left to fend and play for themselves.

The load in and sound check occurred a few hours earlier. Yet just before the show starts, the technician casually mentions that they've turned the levels up "'cause it needs to be really loud," so now it's anyone's guess how anything will sound. Also, a new PA system just got installed that morning, so the performers are about to discover all its kinks live.

This audience is a sea of faces – curious, open, indefatigable – who after two hours of listening still seem to want more.

The performer weaves their way to the stage among anticipating bodies, a taut string of nerves and volatile vibrations, temporarily separating themselves from the rest of the room, shedding the figure of spectator and donning the mantle of player.

This audience is a bar of regulars who've come more for the beer and a chance to shine at the open mic afterwards than the poetry. This audience is an art-and-music crowd who won't be afraid to show their interest or lack of it.

Just before the first note is played, the first syllable mouthed, the first sound sounded, a suspended moment, an entreaty, avowal, petition, declaration for connection with the room. Then the plunge, a reckless dive, a surrender to the moment with conviction that anything could happen.

This audience is imaginary, virtual, invisible, an abstract number in the corner of the screen. This audience starts out challenging, almost hostile, but gradually mellows out by the end of the night. This audience is a mix of sceptics and enthusiasts, a discerning crowd who'll give frank feedback after the show. This audience may be too good to be true.

Between the audience and the performer, a febrile space they shape together, a constant flow of entries and responses as listening distorts the boundaries of their status (maker/receiver), democratizing them into a room of listeners.

This audience is a picture of politeness, quiet when required, applauding at the indicated moments, watching when encouraged to watch. This audience is telling you, politely, that you've failed to move them in any shape or form.

Mistakes will happen as they invariably do. A track won't play, a wrong button will be pressed, a volume will be off, a sequence will be forgotten. The point is not to see these as "mistakes" but as outcomes of the moment, a kind of opportunity to go in unexpected directions.

From the start, this audience projects a roomful of expectations. From the start, you fear you'll fall short of these expectations, so you begin, predictably, on a disappointing false note. This audience is inscrutable, masters of disguise. This audience will refuse to let you in, minute by painful minute. This audience is skilled at dividing the labour of its listening among its various bodies: close, distracted, active, absent, focused, multifocal, selective, critical, deep, partial, relational ...

The end entails another suspended moment – before the protocol of applause kicks in – a moment in which the connection that's been established – excited, moved, indifferent, inspired, curious, puzzled – is confirmed.

This audience is very generous, puts on a brave face despite the awkward cramped space, the badly lit stage, the hissing speaker, the glitchy mic. This audience is agitated and here to have fun, damn it! This audience is determined to keep things light and airy. This audience, composed largely of your friends, is forgiving and will support-applaud you no matter how off you might be tonight.

The performer's final act is to leave the stage, rejoin the audience for the next and the next, and so ensure that the cycle continues.

CHAMBERSONIC :
POROUS SEUIL POSSIBLE SOLO

After (Octavian Nemescu's *Pourras-tu seul?*, a score for imaginary music) and Before (an imaginary score)

The score partitioned as meditation, the music impossible to sound and thus resonating, amplifying in the inner ear, in the ether, in the chaotic, polyform, fluctuating space of the mind, in an instant, an hour, a decade, a lifetime. Whose lifetime? you might ask. The insect's? The tree's? The human's? The erratic's? The planet's? To outlive the sound and become its derivative, be obstinate, insistent on its wildness, the agency of its voicing, its refusal to be controlled, technically mastered. What follows, and therefore what comes before, revels in the fallible yet joyous pursuit of the amateur, the dabbling soloist poised on the porous threshold between sound and its absence.

Montréal, 2024
almost 5,000 miles away, almost 50 years later

imagine the notation as

the pitter-patter of a spider inching on damp earth

the muffled motion of a jellyfish retreating in the distance

the frantic flapping of a moth's wings against a lightbulb

imagine this sonic amalgam as the whim
                                        glue of your existence

imagine a space, an empty room perhaps
open to a universe of sonic/auditory possibilities

where you can harness this sound
be its spectre

become its breath through all your senses, all your pores, all your
nerve endings, all your follicles, all your muscles, all your
magnetic energy, all your water, all your electricity, all your
synaptic firing, all the micro movements of your bones, all your
hues, all your tones, all your breath,

which e x pa n d in g and contracting becomes

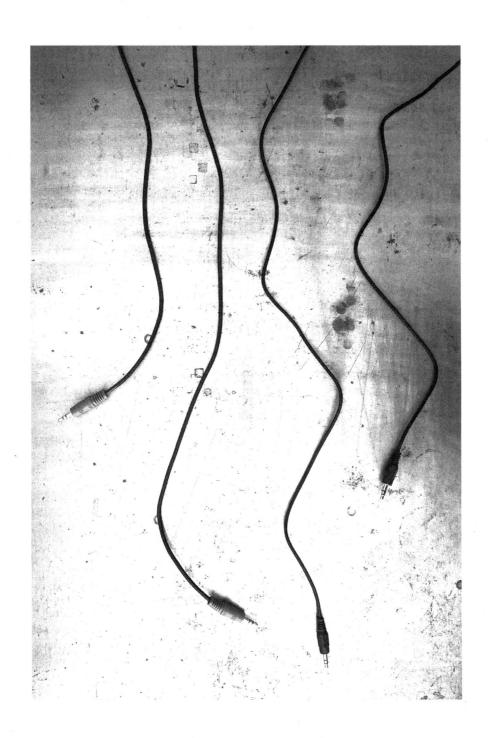

the sound

   of the slow, persistent, millennial, frank, constant, submerged

      friction

    of tectonic plates

solid rock grinding against solid rock

   sediment depositing over sediment

a subducted music of an entire planet living as

   an enormous unfathomable percussive instrument

that reverberates outwards

    beyond the humus
          the oceans
        the troposphere
           the stratosphere
        the mesosphere
           the thermosphere

to the satellite sounds

of hundreds of languages, thousands of voices, millions of
accents, billions of data, numbers, images

orbiting
translating
pulsing
transmitting

radio waves
descending
plummeting
striking
bouncing off

land-tethered abeyant antennas

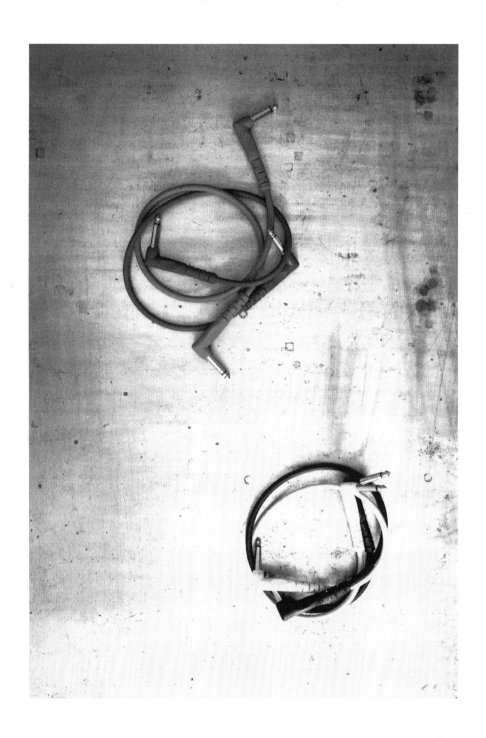

but also imagine these same sounds

    as the interlude (parenthesis) of your   jouissance
    seeded by the reiterative breath
    of all you inhale   encounter incorporate
    and let germinate in you
                  all the

            particles
            frequencies
            spectrums
            discourses
            memories

    and the reiterative breath
    of all you exhale   release generate
    and propagate into

            memories
            discourses
            spectrums
            frequencies
            particles

which are both what make you
and what is made by you

an interlude that is also sharp, metallic, irregular

    ping   of sonar   encountering
                  ocean
                      floor

mixed with the gentle rubbing
of a hollow rod of chrome

that keeps approaching a melodic pitch
  yet remains a soft dry rasping friction
                a perpetual reaching towards

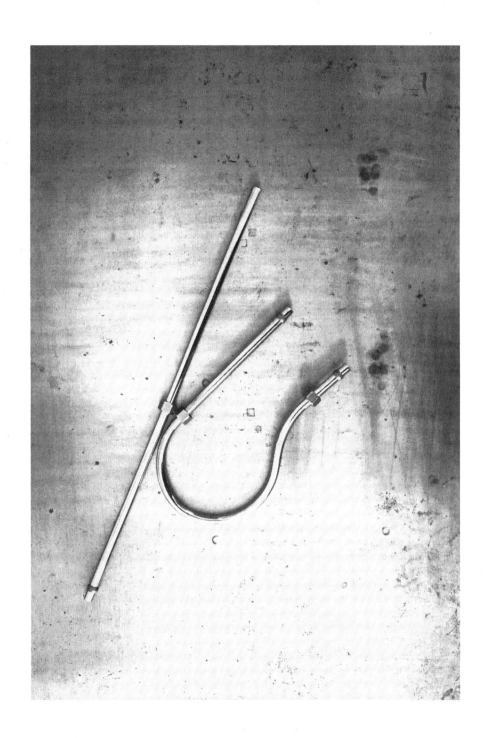

the imaginary inductive sound
that you don   inhabit like a cocoon
                    in which you place

            your ethics
                your biomes
                    your conjectures
                        your inconsistencies
                        your filaments
                            your contradictions
                            your anomalies

        so that through this imaginary sonic cocoon
        you might broadcast (even if only for a fleeting
        instance) a kind of humble entanglement

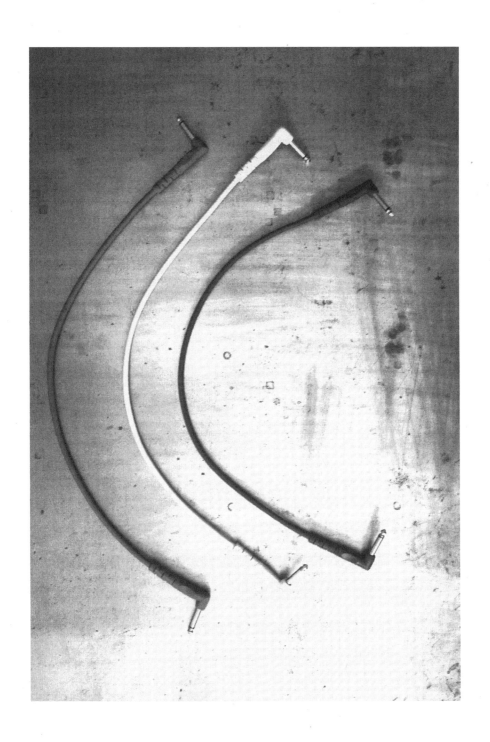

of sonic notes as harbours
      as incandescent presences

      in the room turned grotto turned arena turned coliseum

become gong and pluck and bow and beat and string and tap

vibrate into the low steady hum of electricity
drip into ink diluting in a pool of water

      with all your senses
    all your pores
  all your nerve endings
      all your synapses
    all your tones

i   n   u   n   d   a   t   e

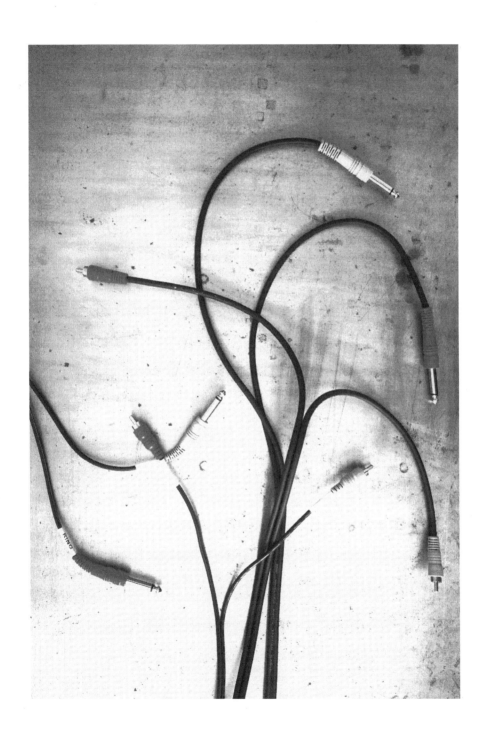

the chorus of sediments rooting over millennia
cacophonies of far-off astral bodies
throat caught in mid swallow
mid note
mid utterance

all pouring into
the echo chamber
of the mind

the babble of
blood   sap   water

the tuning fork
of your noise
and silence

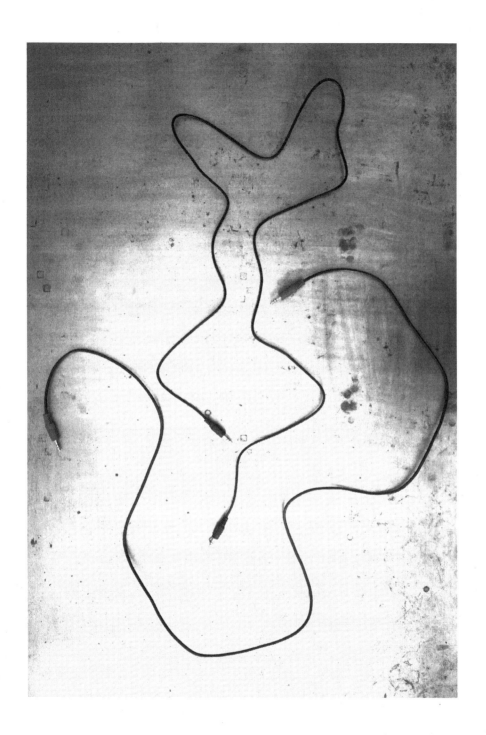

CHAMBERSONIC :
SILENCES

This (   ) is a mitigation of circumstance.

This (   ) is an operatic meteor, an allegory of unfacts.

This (   ) is a sonic breath, extended into an embodied yes.

This (   ) is the future fully activated in the present.

This (   ) is timesense, sensorientation, intensuality.

This (   ) is a description of an utterance, an urgent cry, a conflagration, a
                                                        symphonic assembly.

This (   ) is a now in dialogue, a system of beyonds, befores, begones.

This (   ) is an unsigned affidavit, a gossip.

This (   ) is intentionality as only possible in dreams.

This (   ) is a fact gone off the rails, off the books, off-kilter.

This (   ) is an injection into the senses.

This (   ) is awakening, expanding in the zone.

This (   ) is a nonlecture, improbable performance, out-of-order catalogue.

This (   ) is politico-, umbilico-, philosophico-, economico-, syllabico-
wordbrewing, worldmaking.

This (   ) is shacking up with adversaries, misunderstandings, inquiries.

This (   ) is betwixt the temperaments.

This (   ) is taking the temperature of one's inner weather, one's excessive
environment.

This (   ) is a calling to a voicing, a making.

This (   ) is a window.

This (   ) is a visionary presence, an enchantment.

This (   ) is an articulated way of being, a responsive ethics.

This (   ) is a biome.

This (   ) is urgent, non-negotiable.

This (   ) is a multitude of solitudes, swarm of amplitudes, animal
amplification, echoes wandering back, defiant.

CHAMBERSONIC : DISCORDANT CHORDS

A revolution sits on the tip of a tongue

a moral quandary on the tip of another

here an incursion   there an indictment

unspoken   held in

for the moment choosing (is it a choice?)

to remain internal

perhaps out of passivity

a failure of impetus

Yet the revolution is fuming   voices pollinate

and splinter

the incursion is gasping   grasping for

a dangerous and willful moment

in a history never meant for children

Addicted to its own necessity   climate of whispers

articulations

the quandary is ignored   undocumented   invisible

while an overriding popular track plays on repeat

plays on repeat

plays on repeat

everywhere outside the mouth   plays on repeat

plays on repeat

The tip of the tongue is precocious
digital realms
a thought away from slipping into the mire

The tip of the tongue wants

distractions questions textures flavours skin air a public life

The tip of the tongue pushes syllables out
wounds inattention
vocalizations exclamations emphatic rehearsals breath

Figure of the uttered and the unsaid
audible flows
a stance about to shift into action

the tip of the tongue is precarious

a breath away from tipping into the abyss
a slap a doubt
the vortex spun by one-sided social prowess

A day comes to face the music

allow some spillage

the fickle moods tuned to headlines

predictable   yet vibrating

almost on the verge of understanding

The day is will be a mercurial albatross or phoenix
assailed melody

Only the continual now can decide
tenuous creature

The day was now   centuries ago   eons from now

a figment of the margins
tongues in the mire
a thorn in the entrenchments of centre
feet in the way
a sudden reflex of an outstretched hand

An I lingers in the harbour of a late spring
scatters in the sightlines of an early and murderous autumn
opalesces in the mine of fatal convictions
An I deals in mercury and borax   petroleum and polonium
coltan and lithium
transits in vulnerable bodies   enforced displacement

An I platitudes   vociferates   speaks for
or goes along with the status quo
An I sees and pretends not to see
hears and pretends not to hear
An I capitulates because it's easy to follow along
An I repeats
in different eras   languages   bodies   wars

sleepless nights of terror
O constricted throat

o thorax and tongue   esophagus and amygdala

severed even before a first breath is uttered

or divergent thought made possible

a future target
The vulnerable body betrayed by the body politic
scrambling about
The human body severed
on the move in the dark
the whale body severed

the elephant body severed

the bear body   the wolf body   the fox body   the snake body

the cicada body   the bee body   the aspen body   the maple body

the birch body   the bulrush body   the plantain body   the echinacea body

the thistle body   the limestone body   the iron body   the coal body

the salt body   the water molecule body   the astral dust body

the magnetic body   the gravitational body severed

At what cost the murmuring along the borders? the blurred topography
The building of walls?   restless
The shelling of the demarcations? restless
Into what crack does a slippery margin fall? restless
Or fail?   restless
Can reverberation be a kind of active entreaty? restless
How can a mouth sing when hovering over a widening crater of loss?
Yet some attunement must be found

An I stands on the shore of itself

If in removing the gag   creating an echo

an I looks for shifts and small divergences

the continual reshaping

the dust in the winds

reimagining of connections with everything not I

the questions in the noise

Such shifts can become collaborations with environment

an understood entente

Bodies acting as hinges

or verbs in the syntax of environment

An I might go into the syntax with a wild desire to scar

or shed its formulas

It might be vulnerable to backtracking

inflated to a bullhorn

rehearsals routines

reduced to a mouthpiece parroting contexts

senses temporarily distracted   closed to you

its interlocutors

You go into its syntax full of purpose

a trusting openness to the porous membranes

of planetary dynamics   flickers of the asters

sap   heartbeat   hand

treble of an ordinary morning

attuned to interstitial forces

simply present

So an I might learn

to slow

to quiet

to listen with

Against the bureaucratic snarls drowning out those locked inside the gates
you call on the multitude of irreconcilable tongues
mouths of lichen and animal tracks in the snow
mouths of faded cerulean sky filtering through pale grey branches
mouths of spring runoff and the sharp clean odour of damp earth
mouths gluttonous and feral
mouths denuded and choral
mouths quiet yet disobedient
guttural mouths   soft-spoken mouths   irreverent mouths   illiterate mouths
hybrid mouths   high-pitched mouths   baritone mouths   dainty mouths
full-lipped mouths   sensual mouths   disoriented mouths   dirty mouths
eloquent mouths   expectant mouths   repulsed mouths   reawakened mouths
plurilingual mouths   working mouths   itinerant mouths   wandering mouths
gutter mouths   rebellious mouths   recalcitrant mouths   reasonable mouths
unreasonable mouths   shouting mouths   singing mouths   unobstructed mouths

An I offers its noise and dust

Another its petty concerns

One its deadly conflicts

Another its cosmic angst

The questions are many and lie undigested

Wind bites at their edges

neither indifferent nor concerned

simply present   an I might learn

                         to slow

In the treble of an ordinary morning

social goes to pasture   to quiet

                      to listen with

An I tackles a daily cycle of attempts

It's almost a routine   or a rehearsal

though carried out with a certain amount of rigour

Somewhere the shuffling of paper

Somewhere the staccato drone of a motor

Somewhere a domestic series of gestures

Somewhere a child crying

Somewhere a supersonic blast   a market stall collapsing

Somewhere water cooling the skin of an ardent encounter

Somewhere limbs trapped under rubble

Somewhere the tumble of running shoes in the dryer

Somewhere the cold breath of a quiet moment on a park bench

Somewhere the constant din of rocket fire

There are sites   strata   states

where beginnings are possible

and there are sites where they are not

An I has to wonder the distraction away
         crack the walled murmuring?
will some kind of momentum   some action
         reverberate entreaties into a mouth?
be still and in motion at once
         fall in the margin?
since thought in movement shapes differently
         attune the crater?
depending on the topography

A restless statement hovers in the air

A restless statement tries opening various avenues

For a time the vista remains blurred

visas or certain types of passports required to gain access

such visas only given to those with certain types of passports

The shelter is a hut
an underground chamber   a lean-to with a roof of thatch
a ruin on the outskirts of town
a retreat centre not yet built   a room in the mind
The shelter beckons as a place of refuge   survival
sleepless nights of terror
I you we they shall not fade silently into the night
but leave roaring   marked
betrayed by the body politic
scrambling about in the dark   yes   but at least on the move
The shelter exists in the idea of possible refuge
yet a question nags at the edges
What exactly is refuge?
a bee body
The shelter after all may be just another future target

a birch body
a thistle body
a water body

If an I speaks in tongues

it is because others have tried to excise its tongue of fact

If an I drags its feet through the mire

the glut and rut of inaction

it is because it's slow to mend the mettle of its assailed creature

If an I lingers in the melancholy of an ever-tenuous melody

it is because it has half a mind to crawl and glower its way

deals

to the next millennium

platitudes

    pretends

    capitulates

    repeats

But an I knows that it has to double back and stumble forward

veer off course and doubt and doubt the will of a public life

to gain some semblance of audible clarity

the syllable prowess of tongues

It'll be licking its wounds a hundred times before this is over

It'll be chewing on the dregs of reason before this is put to rights

It'll be masticating digital realms of data (i.e. information for market analysis)

before it can earn its seat at the kids' table

It'll be drowning in inattention   careless distraction   stultifying passivity

before the constant slaps in the face start to become intolerable

It'll be a boy scout   a girl guide   a team player

a confederate   a collaborator   the now of entrenchment

before it realizes that going with the flow just won't do

To become a person

an I needs to stop impersonating

In time an I becomes an echo propelled by its own momentum
lands on the shore (i.e. the threshold) of the shelter
                    A voice booms a quandary
Shoulders bent under the weight
of history (i.e. this moment in the making)
                    A voice stifles a groan a revolution
the moment poised to strike
splinter into a thousand shards of glass
or pollinate a new climate of forms
                    A voice mouths a barely audible whisper an incursion
The shore scatters (i.e. acts as a momentary fracture in a lived past)
                    A voice holds the note of an interminable scream an indictment
Though the shelter might be a mirage casting long shadows over the articulations
a ghostly shimmer or a memory of presence striking in its insistence
Time pounds down disguised as a sudden firestorm
while a strange alchemy transpires between the unspoken and the spoken
                    and a voice awakens

for all the analogue and electronic voices
whose lineage is a never-fading echo

ACKNOWLEDGEMENTS

The epigraph by Theresa Hak Kyung Cha is from her artist book *Audience Distant Relative* (1977); the one by Aldo Clementi from the collection *Notations*, edited by John Cage (Something Else Press, 1969); and the one by Pauline Oliveros from an interview with Tara Rodgers in *Pink Noises* (Duke University Press, 2010).

Chambersonic Intro : Fellow Statements was featured in *Listening, Sound, Agency*, a limited-edition, lathe-cut vinyl produced by Spoken-Web (Concordia University, Montréal, May 2022). **Chambersonic : Let Form Be Oral** was written while reading "Composition as Process: I. Changes, II. Indeterminacy, and III. Communication" by John Cage; its **Movement I** was published in *The Capilano Review*, Issue 3.42: Translingual (Vancouver, Fall 2020). **Chambersonic : Let Form Be Aural** was commissioned by *The Capilano Review* as part of a series of digital activations for their Fall 2020 issue. **Chambersonic : Episodes for an Absent Film** was begun during a residency at OBORO (Montréal, April 2021). **Chambersonic : A Graphic Score** was begun during a residency at CAMAC, Centre d'Art Marnay Art Centre (France, May 2014). **Chambersonic : Living Scores** was commissioned by Blackwood Gallery for *The Society for the Diffusion of Useful Knowledge*, Issue 10: Pronouncing (Mississauga, October 2021). A chapbook of **Chambersonic : Improbable Theatres** was published by Knife Fork Book (Toronto, Summer 2023), while **Theatre Oblique** was commissioned by *The Capilano Review* (Vancouver, Summer 2022). **Chambersonic : Soundpace // Eavesdropping on the Process of a Dilettante Composer** was commissioned by Blackwood Gallery for *SDUK*, Issue 11: Pacing (Mississauga, January 2022). **Chambersonic : Porous Seuil Possible Solo** was commissioned, along with work by Niiqo Pam Dick, by Jumătatea plină for their *Muzica imaginară* project (Romania, 2020) and was published in *OEI* #98-99: Aural Poetics, edited by Michael Nardone (Sweden, Winter 2023). **Chambersonic : Silences** was published in *Columba*, Issue 4 (Summer 2020). Thank you to all the editors, organizers, and curators.

Thank you to the Canada Council for the Arts, OBORO, Ville de Montréal/Centre Culturel Calixa-Lavalée, Le Labo, and CAMAC for their generous support, which gave me the time and space to work on parts of this multiform project.

A few books were particularly inspiring for my thinking in the textual-sonic chamber, including *Silence* by John Cage and *Notations* edited by John Cage, *A Voice and Nothing More* by Mladen Dolar, *Plans for Sentences* by Renee Gladman, *Now that the audience is assembled* by David Grubbs, *A Voice to Perform: One Opera/Two Plays* by Carla Harryman, *Imagined Theatres: Writing for a Theoretical Stage* edited by Daniel Sack, and *Spit Temple* by Cecilia Vicuña. A few equally stimulating sound artists and performers include Magali Babin, Anne-James Chaton, Moe Clark, Christof Migone, Pauline Oliveros, and Pamela Z.

A generous and special thank you to Lou Pam Dick who makes my every day unique with constant inspiration, energizing presence, and invaluable encouragement; to Erín Moure and Chantal Neveu pour leur complicité littéraire et leur amitié, and to Lou Pam and Erín for their vital feedback as the book's first readers; to Stephen Collis for editorial acumen; to Margaret Christakos, Christof Migone, and Zoë Skoulding for their time and words; and to the Talonbooks team, especially Ryan Fitzpatrick, Catriona Strang, Leslie Smith, and Kevin Williams, for bringing this constellation into book form.

Oana Avasilichioaei is a poet-artist, sound performer, and translator interested in polyphonic poetics, phonotophes (intermediary spaces between words, sounds, and images), and states of listening. Distinctions include the A. M. Klein Prize for Poetry, the Cole Foundation Prize for Translation, and the Governor General's Literary Award for Translation. She has been a writer-in-residence at Green College, UBC, and the University of Calgary and an artist-in-residence at Simon Fraser University and OBORO, among others. *Chambersonic* is her seventh book. See oanalab.com.